MW01611171

Self Reflection

A Journey to a Better You

Lindsay Locke

THEA HARRIS PUBLISHING

Thea Harris Publishing, Inc.
Port St Lucie, Florida
Theaharrispublishing.com

This book or parts thereof may not be reproduced in any form, stored in a retrieval system, or transmitted in any form by any means - electronic, mechanical, photocopy, recording or otherwise - without prior written permission of the publisher, except as provided by United States of America copyright law.

Cover Design © 2022 by Quiet Strength Designs

Published by Thea Harris Publishing ~ P.O. Box 7576
Port St. Lucie, FL 34985 ~ www.theaharrispublishing.com.
Copyright © 2022 Lindsay Locke
All rights reserved.
ISBN: 0-9909170-5-3
ISBN- 13: 978-0-9909170-5-2

DEDICATION

This book is dedicated to my daughter Jaelyn Rene Chapman
who always inspired me to chase my dreams.

CONTENTS

Self-reflect to grow and thrive.

- *Lindsay*

Introduction

Personal growth is a never-ending journey that holds the key to overall health and happiness. A desire to grow means we simply refuse to be content with our current circumstances. It's not a sign that we're doing poorly but that we want to do better. This is a wonderful place to start!

Reflecting on flaws and mistakes empowers us to mold ourselves into the people we imagine. Although self-reflection may be challenging, it is essential to truly thrive. If we refuse to look inward due to an unreasonably self-imposed expectation to be perfect, or if we think we already are, it cultivates a mindset that isn't conducive to a journey to being better. Our lives won't change if we never change anything about ourselves.

The power of self-reflection is immeasurable. Evaluating yourself and identifying opportunities for improvement will launch you to higher levels of success and happiness. You will achieve limitless growth in your career and personal life. It may seem discouraging to highlight imperfections, but don't look at it that way. Instead, see this as exciting and uplifting, a chance to strengthen your weaknesses and enhance your strengths.

Self-Reflection: A Journey to a Better You was designed to help you identify areas in life where introspection may increase your overall happiness. It is not just an observational process or tool for assessment but an amazing learning experience in which you will become more self-aware. Your perceptions will change, and positively influence how other people see you. Here is a chance to transform your life, relationships, and outlook for a better quality of living. You attract what you are, so why not take this journey with me? It's time to build a better you.

CHAPTER ONE

Self-Love

The truth is, many people stink at self-love, especially us women.

We completely forget ourselves when we become consumed with caring for and nurturing others. As

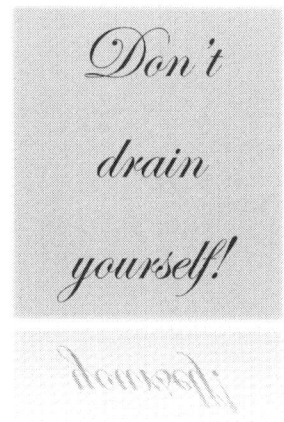

a result, months go by without going to the beauty salon, or more times than not, we skip the gym. Then, we use those gift cards we got for Mother's Day on someone else. Over time, this behavior can cause us to feel neglected, unloved, and unappreciated.

It's okay to be a fountain of love to those around you, but don't drain yourself. Get your hair done. Rest when you need it. Take time to exercise. Buy the things you want, and don't feel guilty. You deserve it! Most importantly, do not wait for other people to pour into you because sometimes, it never happens. Instead, fill your love cup and allow the love others show you to be the topping.

Reflections

What are some of the ways I show self-love?

_____

_____

_____

_____

_____

How can I love myself more?

_____

_____

_____

_____

_____

CHAPTER TWO

Self-Affirmations

Take a moment each morning before you log into that social media account and start comparing yourself to the sometimes-fake images people display of themselves and tell yourself you're awesome.

Society and social media have driven us to this approval and acceptance-seeking obsession

where we thrive off likes and compliments. Don't depend on this for your self-confidence because it is a setup for disappointment. Approve yourself! Accept yourself! Compliment yourself! Impress yourself! You know you better than anyone else, so why not toot your own horn?

Be proud that you are good at what you do. Appreciate your shimmery eyes or radiant skin tone. Remind yourself that you are a good cook or great at crafts. Don't forget the time you put that desk together with no help or started up the BBQ pit all by yourself. Let it be known; you are the best shower singer who's ever walked the earth, and you can untangle a knot in a necklace or shoestring in five seconds flat. Be your source of confidence and your biggest fan. After all, you are amazing!

Reflections

What am I good at?

_____

_____

_____

_____

_____

Write five daily self-affirmations about your abilities

_____

_____

_____

_____

_____

CHAPTER THREE

Self-Security

Some people have insecurities because of how others loved them in their childhood or adult relationships.

Some parents didn't show unconditional love. Adult relationships may have left us feeling hurt

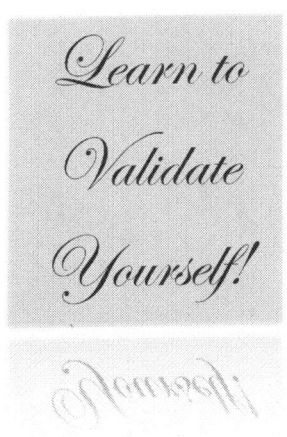

and betrayed. We cannot allow this to make us insecure and in constant need of reassurance. It will negatively affect our relationships and can be an annoyance.

Sure, people may add joy to our lives, but our happiness should not depend on their acceptance. After all, they can leave us at any moment, unexpectedly or by choice. Learn to validate yourself. Actively practice self-security. Let your happiness and confidence come from within. Never allow it to hinge on others' actions or approval. No one or thing is promised to us or guaranteed to be permanent. So, always be your main source of security and confidence.

What makes me insecure?

_____

_____

_____

_____

_____

How can I validate myself more?

_____

_____

_____

_____

_____

CHAPTER FOUR

Confidence

The tricky thing about confidence is that we sometimes don't realize it's missing.

You look in the mirror at home and feel pretty good about yourself, but as soon as you walk into

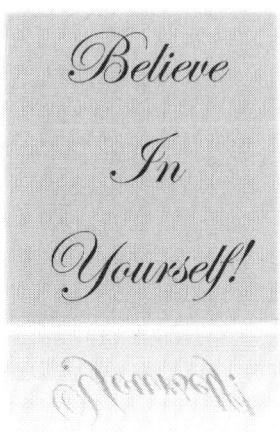

a room with more than five people, you become unsure. You suddenly wonder if your makeup looks cakey or if your shirt compliments your breasts and waistline. You get extremely nervous on the way to job interviews even though you know you're overqualified. You need to call your best friend for support as you drive to that first date you've been looking forward to for weeks.

Our confidence levels may fluctuate, and that's okay. We are human. We shouldn't lose sight of who we are or who we were created to be. Let's walk with confidence, talk with confidence, and most importantly, think confidently. If we don't believe in ourselves, how can we expect anyone else to believe in us?

A lack of confidence often stems from an absence of something else that we haven't addressed. Whether it's a fear of public speaking, limited knowledge, or insecurity, it's up to us to change it. But first, we must ask ourselves what we can improve to be more confident. We become what we believe. So, let's get to work!

Reflections

Where am I most confident?

_____

_____

_____

_____

_____

Where do I lack confidence?

_____

_____

_____

_____

_____

What can I change to become more confident?

_____

_____

_____

_____

_____

~ Write a personal reflection here ~

_____

_____

_____

_____

_____

_____

_____

CHAPTER FIVE

Courage

Sometimes the words courage and courageous are misunderstood or misused. For example, you may think you have to be fearless to have courage. You couldn't be more wrong.

Courage doesn't indicate the absence of fear but a willingness and bravery to face it head-on! For

example, you may be afraid of heights. The challenge will make you uncomfortable, but you won't grow if you don't face your fears.

The first step is to admit you're scared. Own it and know that if you are, it's okay. Next, remember you were created to be strong and courageous and tap into your confidence. Finally, face your fear! Some things take baby steps, and that is okay. You may need to overcome other things in one giant leap. Regardless, remember you can be both scared and courageous. Without fear, you will never find your courage.

Reflections

What are my fears?

_____

_____

_____

_____

What can I do to overcome them?

_____

_____

_____

_____

_____

CHAPTER SIX

Forgive Others

Life is full of unexpected events, plot twists, and surprises, but one thing you can count on is that people will hurt you.

It sounds horrible, but it's the truth. People will disappoint you, betray your trust, insult you, steal

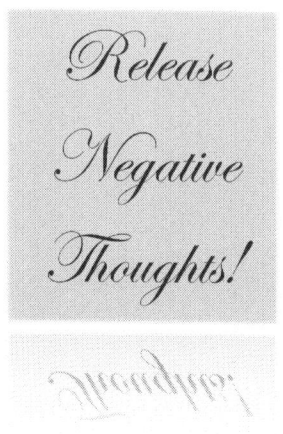

from you, lie to you, and the list goes on and on. You set certain expectations of others, and when they don't meet those expectations, you usually end up hurt or angry. It's okay to feel that way and to communicate this to them. It is acceptable to remove them from your life if it brings you peace. Just remember, don't hold grudges. Instead, release resentments and use that energy to nurture another relationship.

Forgiving someone doesn't mean you have to be their friend. It requires that you let go of negative thoughts that consume your mind and the poisonous words you speak. Replace them with positivity. You have a limited volume of energy; use it wisely. Forgive!

Reflections

What grudges am I holding on to?

_____

_____

_____

_____

_____

What steps can I take to forgive?

_____

_____

_____

_____

_____

CHAPTER SEVEN

Forgive Yourself

Oh, you think forgiving others is hard? Sometimes we are harder on ourselves than we are on anyone else.

Try forgiving yourself for dropping out of high school or missing out on that college scholarship.

Try forgiving yourself for messing up relationships or for those irreversible parenting mistakes. Let them go.

Guess what? You can't undo anything from the past! You can never go back in time. You can't unscramble scrambled eggs! What's done is done, and it's time to let it go.

Free yourself from the prison of self-punishment. Remove the shackles of shame and lift your head with pride. The anger you feel is an acknowledgment of mistakes. Acknowledgment is the first step, and most people aren't even willing to do that much. Next, identify the lesson in the experience. Take what you learned and use it as a building block to a better you. Finally, forgive yourself. No one is perfect; no one navigates life without making mistakes - and mistakes are different depending on the journey. The lessons you learn make you who you are; they sculpt who you become.

Reflections

What have I not forgiven myself for?

_____

_____

_____

_____

_____

What steps can I take to forgive myself?

_____

_____

_____

_____

_____

CHAPTER EIGHT

Reacting

Things happen that are beyond our control, but we can decide how we react to them.

We endure disappointments, failures, betrayal, rejection, loss, and hardships, some of which are  not our fault. We cannot let unfortunate circumstances define us. They should not determine our future. We can, however, be accountable for how we react to these situations. Unfortunately, it's reactions that can get us into a pickle. Ultimately, we control our actions and responses. So, check that temper, and stabilize those emotions.

Never make significant choices when you are in an extreme emotional state. These are not decisions, they are reactions, and you may regret them later. Calm down, think, and consider what will happen because of how you reacted. Separate feelings from facts to help you control your responses to things and people. You cannot let your feelings outweigh the truth when making important choices. Calm, cool, calculated decisions beat emotional outbursts any day!

Reflections

In what situation could I have reacted better?

_____

_____

_____

_____

_____

What steps can I take to ensure healthy responses?

_____

_____

_____

_____

_____

CHAPTER NINE

Emotional Stability

Let's be honest; stabilizing emotions is not always easy!
After all, emotions are powerful!

Obtaining and maintaining emotional stability can be hard work, and that's okay. It doesn't make

you bad or mentally ill because you are sensitive. Never let anyone make you feel that way. You cannot let your emotions take over. Emotions are perfectly normal when processing difficult experiences. It's when you lose control that it becomes unhealthy. Recognize and acknowledge when you begin feeling a shift or change and allow yourself to process. Sometimes it's best to take a little time alone. It could be thirty minutes or a day or two. Do whatever you need to examine what you feel without projecting it on anyone else.

Identify the root cause of your emotions. It is so important! The surface cause is not always the same as the root cause. For example, someone said something that offended you - surface, but the root cause could be that you take things personally when you shouldn't. Identify both.

Focus on a solution to your feelings. The fix may be a simple conversation. Distancing yourself from someone might be the answer. People are who they are, and sometimes it has nothing to do with you, so don't take things personally. If the way someone treats you causes unhealthy emotions, perhaps you need to accept that who they are doesn't suit your life in a good way. Often, the first step in working toward emotional stability is walking away from toxic people, environments, and relationships. Set boundaries! Finally, actively work to control your feelings.

Reflections

Which of my emotions sometimes take over in an unhealthy way?

_____

_____

_____

_____

Is there a specific person or environment that triggers this?

_____

_____

_____

_____

_____

What can I do to actively control my feelings?

_____

_____

_____

_____

_____

~ Write a personal reflection here ~

_____

_____

_____

_____

_____

_____

_____

_____

CHAPTER TEN

Love

Love, love, love. Where do I start?

There are misconceptions surrounding love. Some believe it is tough or painful, confusing, or

complicated. We tell ourselves flat-out lies to justify others' actions or our own decisions. Love is simple, pure, and beautiful. We make it difficult and painful.

You cannot control what other people do, but you can manage your decisions and actions. Unhealthy situations create confusion and complications – like continuously allowing people to hurt or disappoint you or staying in one-sided, unfair relationships. When you separate facts from feelings, it helps simplify your perception of love.

Love is supposed to be our medicine, our therapy, not become the reason we need a therapist. It should make us feel supported and appreciated, not alone and neglected. Love is not something we have to chase or wait for; it flows freely and gracefully. It doesn't have conditions or unfair expectations.

Be honest with yourself about love, but most importantly, be realistic about other people's actions around it. Love yourself enough to identify what or who is hurting you. It's usually you, not love. Don't put or keep yourself in situations that wound you, then say love hurts!

Reflections

Do I feel like love is hurting me?

_____

_____

_____

_____

_____

What or who hurts me?

_____

_____

_____

_____

_____

What can I do to stop it?

_____

_____

_____

_____

_____

What are some healthy ways I give and receive love?

_____

_____

_____

_____

_____

CHAPTER ELEVEN

Exercise

Mental and physical health work together. Most people who don't exercise avoid it because it seems overwhelming. That's why getting started is the hardest part!

You don't have to run a mile on your first day at the track or do 100 sit-ups right away to start

trimming that belly fat. If you are a beginner, own it and set reasonable goals. For example, don't plan to lose thirty pounds in three months if you are thirty pounds overweight. Be careful not to let the larger or longer-term goal be your main focus. Set smaller, more attainable objectives - like losing three pounds per week.

Long-term goals are not wrong, but you can create unrealistic expectations by comparing yourself to some workout model you saw on

YouTube. It's great to focus on short-term goals and celebrate small victories as you achieve them. It's not always about how you look; it's about how you feel; it's about adding years to your life.

Exercise increases endorphins in your brain, which can help you deal with things like stress, anxiety, and depression. Your body is your temple, the only one you have. It is your vehicle, and you should treat it as such. Would you feel better riding around in a foreign luxury car or a broken-down hooptie?

Reflections

What exercises do I enjoy?

_____

_____

_____

_____

Who might like to exercise with me?

_____

_____

_____

_____

How can I make time to exercise?

_____

_____

_____

_____

_____

Exercise goals

_____

_____

_____

_____

_____

CHAPTER TWELVE

Parenting

If you ever need to read instructions on how to complete a challenging task correctly, parenting is probably it! But unfortunately, it doesn't come with a how-to manual or even a warning label.

A child is born into this world, then BOOM, you're a parent, and you have to figure it out as you go. It

starts with diapers and diarrhea. Then, it's puberty and driving lessons, with a whole lot of stress, love, and uncertainty in between. You fight every day to find a balance between parent and friend, guidance and trust, protection and allowing growth, structure, and freedom.

You try your best to shield your children from the world and prevent them from making the same mistakes you did. You steer them down the right path or what you think is the right path for them. They go through these stages where you don't think they are grateful for a single thing you've ever done or listened to anything you've said. Then, they make you so proud that your heart just rockets out of your chest with excitement!

There is no perfection in parenting. There will be mistakes and things you are unsure of how to handle. You won't always have the answers. Parenting is one thing you must genuinely give your best shot. Like anything else in life, it is a learning experience with endless opportunities for growth. Don't pressure yourself to be the perfect parent. Instead, encourage yourself to be a progressing parent.

Reflections

What things do I do well as a parent?

_____

_____

_____

_____

_____

What things can I improve?

_____

_____

_____

_____

_____

What steps will I take to improve?

_____

_____

_____

_____

_____

~ Write a personal reflection here ~

_____

_____

_____

_____

_____

_____

_____

_____

CHAPTER THIRTEEN

Patience

If you are like most people, you know what you want and you want it now, especially when it is related to what you are passionate about!

We can be impatient about love, finances, or our careers most of the time. But we must realize,

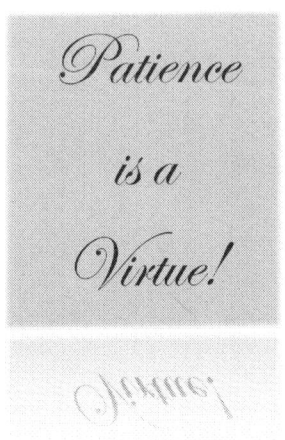

things that come quickly and easily are often temporary because they typically lack a strong foundation.

Allow them to flow and grow, naturally, with time. Rushing can backfire and we will end up back at square one - right where we started. If we keep repeating this cycle, we become drained and discouraged and may even choose to give up anyway.

Don't cheat yourself by being impatient. There are many cliché sayings to reference this, such as "patience is a virtue "or "good things come to those who wait," but "the proof is in the pudding!" Take a moment to think back on your life. Which situations or relationships did you rush into, and which of them are still standing today? Reflect on that; build things brick by brick, layer by layer, and lesson by lesson. Don't settle for something that comes quickly and miss out on the longevity in the reward due to a lack of patience.

Reflections

What am I impatient about?

_____

_____

_____

_____

_____

How can I be more patient with these things?

_____

_____

_____

_____

_____

CHAPTER FOURTEEN

Accountability

Hold on; this was a good book until someone said accountability. Right? But accountability is necessary if you want to build a better you.

We must be accountable for our actions [mistakes, decisions, behavior, goals, habits, words,

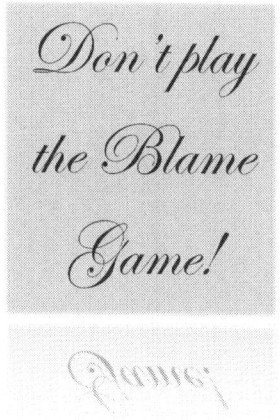

and future]. Don't play the blame game! Things happened that couldn't be prevented or controlled. Do we allow them to dictate our future? How do we respond to them? By taking responsibility for the choices we make in these situations. That could mean breaking a family cycle of addiction, poverty, or changing our diet instead of focusing on the things we blame for our weight gain.

Look for purpose in the pain of a tragedy. When you are accountable, you admit what you've done wrong and reflect on what you can do to be better. No one is perfect! Everyone can improve and grow in some way. Start journaling if you feel overwhelmed about being accountable or don't know where to begin. This will help identify and organize your goals. It is also a guide for following through on those plans. Persevering is perhaps the most critical part.

Have you started something and not seen it to the end? An accountability partner assists by helping you remain consistent because they help you feel supported. They also motivate you to stay focused because you have someone else to answer to besides yourself.

❖

Reflections

What are some unfortunate circumstances in my life?

_____

_____

_____

_____

_____

How have I responded to them?

_____

_____

_____

_____

_____

What can I do to be accountable in those situations?

_____

_____

_____

_____

_____

~ Write a personal reflection here ~

_____

_____

_____

_____

_____

_____

_____

_____

CHAPTER FIFTEEN

Emotional Intelligence

It's one thing to be intelligent but emotional intelligence can elevate you to a new level.

Understanding our emotions and the emotions of others will improve every aspect of our lives,

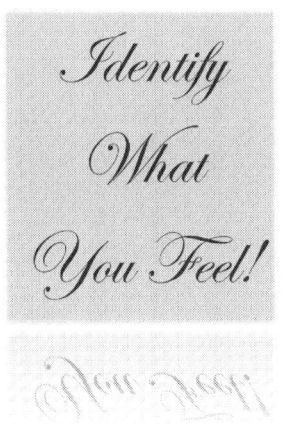

including personally and professionally. We control our actions and reactions when we identify our feelings and, more importantly, why we feel them.

Additionally, identifying and being considerate of others' feelings is key to maintaining healthy relationships. Of course, I'm not saying we should live our lives according to how others think of us. So, let me clarify.

49

Have you ever heard the saying, "People may not remember what you said or what you did, but they'll always remember how you made them feel?" Be considerate of how your actions and words affect others. Relate to them well every chance you get. Be part of why they feel good and excited about life. All you do leaves an impression on others. Leave a legacy of love.

Reflections

What emotions do I sometimes feel very strongly, and what triggers them?

_____

_____

_____

_____

_____

How can I help others feel good?

_____

_____

_____

_____

_____

CHAPTER SIXTEEN

Individuality

In today's world of social media influencers and celebrity lives on display for society, it's easy to fall into the trap of wanting to be like someone else.

Whether it's the way our bodies look, our hair texture, social status, or abilities and talents, we

must embrace who we are! Stop comparing your waistline to that model's or your voice to that singer's. Quit obsessing over your lips, chin, or the tone or clarity of your skin. If you were meant to be any different than you are now, you would have been created that way. Society has done a good job of brainwashing us into a comparison mindset, and it is unhealthy.

Half of what you see of others from a distance is a lie anyway. While it's okay to recognize and appreciate another person's successes, accomplishments, and outstanding attributes, don't put anyone on a pedestal. No one is better than you! People's uniqueness and individuality make the world go round. There is not, and never will be, another you. So, wear your identity proudly and well!

Reflections

What is unique about me?

_____

_____

_____

_____

_____

What do I love about myself?

_____

_____

_____

_____

_____

CHAPTER SEVENTEEN

Setting Goals

We have desires and dreams about things we want to achieve.

We lie in bed at night and think or daydream at our desks all day about who we want to become,

things we want to do or places we want to go. Often, however, we just don't know where to start. It can all be so overwhelming. We must have an action plan that clearly outlines the starting point to the finish line and defines each step in between.

A goal can be anything that differs from the current state of being in health, career, financial, or personal, such as traveling. Goal setting is a significant part of building a better you; in fact, it is a goal in itself – one that is broad but attainable.

The best way to start setting a goal is to be specific, like saving money or losing weight. Map out exactly how much money you want to save or decide how much weight you want to lose within a specific period. Then set even more specific goals with shorter timeframes to map out how you will progress toward your ultimate goal. Also, keep track of your goals and thoughts about them by writing them down.

After that, organize the ideas surrounding your goals and your plans to achieve them. Thoughts can sometimes be chaotic because they bring on doubt and fear. When you begin to experience these thoughts write down opposing statements to counteract them. Be specific about your goals, be intentional with your thoughts, and be accountable for your actions.

Reflections

What three goals do I want to set?

_____

_____

_____

_____

_____

What positive thoughts can I cultivate about accomplishing them?

_____

_____

_____

_____

_____

What steps will I take to reach those goals, including timeframes and smaller goals along the way?

_____

_____

_____

_____

_____

~ Write a personal reflection here ~

_____

_____

_____

_____

_____

_____

_____

CHAPTER EIGHTEEN

Organization

To be quite honest, I'm probably the last person that should be telling others how to be organized! But hey, this book is about building a better you. I'm building too!

We're on this journey together! I've heard it said that the way you organize your closet mirrors your life. Go, look in yours and think about it for a moment. Are your things in order? Are there designated places for your clothes and shoes, or are they just wherever you tossed them? Now think about your life. Are people where they should be? Do you have your priorities in order? Are your goals and plans mapped out? Have you placed your important belongings where they

should be, or are you frequently searching for things?

When it comes to the people in your life, organize them. Know what role each person plays and keep them at appropriate distances. Don't allow people in and out of your life, wreaking havoc and then leaving it destroyed, like a messy closet. Also, keep your priorities in order. Make to-do lists. Itemize your bills and when they are due.

Give quality time to loved ones. Be productive about your health and goals and spend the right amount of time relaxing. Keep essential things in a designated place so they are easy to find when you need them. It can be as simple as getting a key rack to organize keys or as specific as a safety deposit box for important or valuable items. Organizing sets the best tone daily for your mind and your life. Time to clean out our closets!

Reflections

What people or things in my life can I organize or prioritize better?

_____

_____

_____

_____

_____

What specific steps can I take to accomplish this?

_____

_____

_____

_____

_____

CHAPTER NINETEEN

Consistency

It is easy to start something new. Come on; you're all revved up and ready to go!

You've got a flame burning inside you that has you more motivated than ever. You get started, and you're super focused. Then life starts to happen. The kids have homework and soccer games. The house needs cleaning, and the laundry isn't going to wash itself. Work is hectic. You're so tired you are in bed by 9:00 pm most days just to wake up and do everything again.

Before you know it, you are distracted and off-track - you haven't worked out in weeks or gotten your business plan together. You've forgotten all about that new budget you created to help you save money. The spare minutes you have in a day might be spent sleeping in or watching your favorite show on Netflix. There is nothing wrong with that now and then. Just remember to make time for those goals you set a month ago.

Keep that flame burning inside of you by staying committed to your goals. Discipline is key. You will have to sacrifice sleep, tv time, or even fun sometimes. Accomplishing goals and dreams means sacrificing what we find pleasurable, but the ultimate reward is on the other side!

Reflections

What are some goals I set where I've been inconsistent?

_____

_____

_____

_____

_____

What can I do, change, or sacrifice to stay on track?

_____

_____

_____

_____

_____

CHAPTER TWENTY
Setting Boundaries

Stop allowing people to get away with hurting you or not contributing to your happiness.

Think of a mansion with an expensive car in a lavish neighborhood. Now visualize the surround-

ings. See a security gate to monitor who comes in and out of the area. There is a garage so no one can steal or vandalize the car. Now think about your life. What boundaries do you have in place to protect yourself? How do you safeguard your peace and mental health from outside sources that can easily steal, kill, and destroy them? What do you do to regulate who has access to you?

It is crucial to set boundaries because the harsh reality is people will enter your life with ill intentions and no consideration of your feelings or peace. Family members may take you for granted. Your employer will exhaust you. Friends can take advantage of you, but only to the extent that you allow it. Therefore, it is up to you to set boundaries.

Don't say yes when you know you will most likely end up hurt or disappointed. Instead, start saying, "No." Delete and block people on social media. Put up your security gate and close your garage when you know people have a history of vandalizing you. Setting boundaries makes you accountable for your happiness.

Reflections

In what areas of my life do I lack boundaries?

_____

_____

_____

_____

_____

How can I start setting boundaries to protect myself?

_____

_____

_____

_____

_____

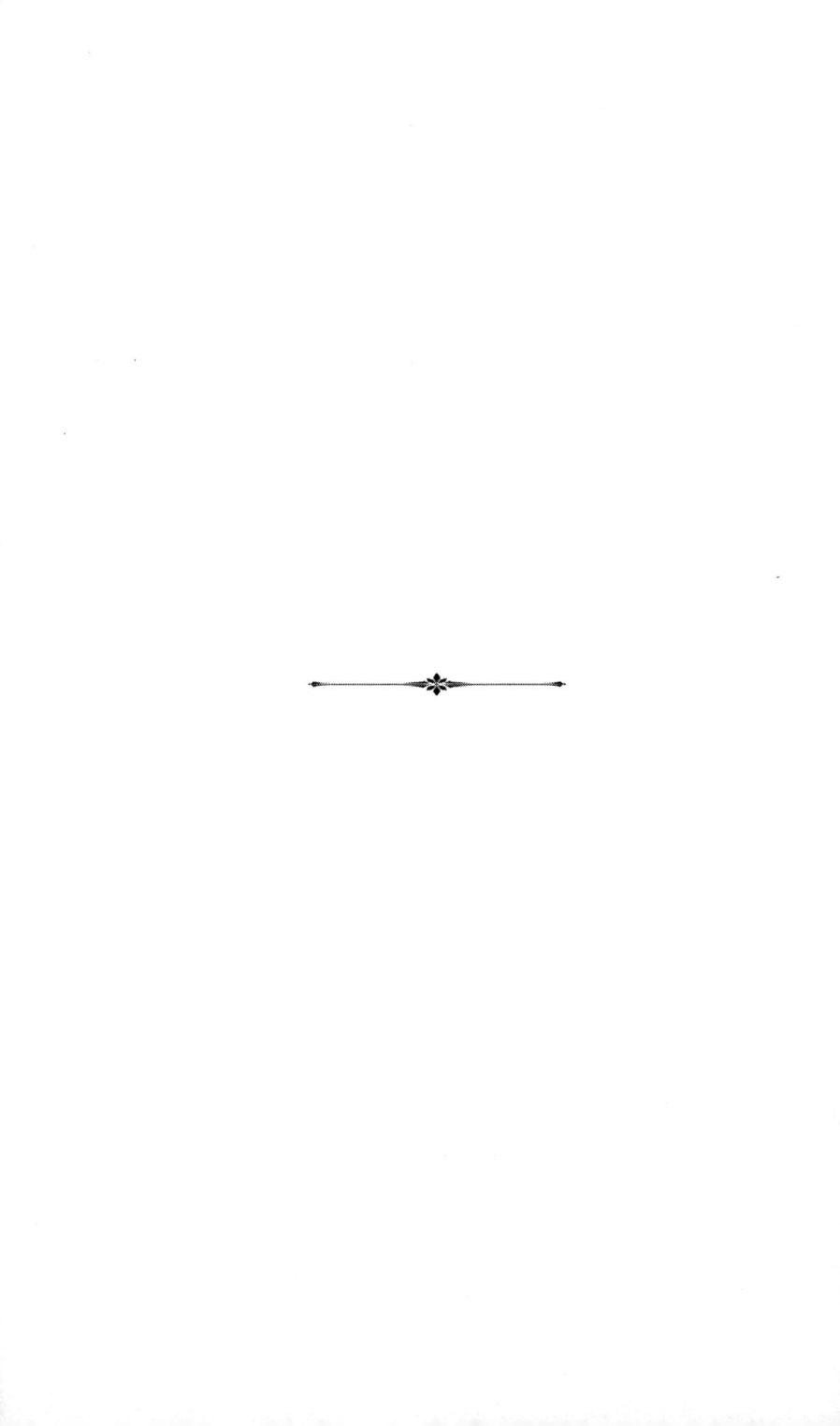

Visit Lockedinforlife.com for
More Information

Follow on Social Media

Instgram.com/Lindsay_Locked_In
Facebook.com/Lindsay LockedIn

ABOUT THE AUTHOR

Lindsay Locke is a Life Coach whose unique purpose is to use her experiences to help others prevail through adversity. Her transformation from high school dropout to a professional leader with a bachelor's degree in Behavioral Science and a master's degree in Business Administration has equipped her to serve her community as a mentor to young girls and women. Lindsay believes self-reflection and accountability are the keys to resilience and improved quality of life. She is the founder of Locked-In Life Coaching and Luv Locked, a youth-focused Nonprofit. Lindsay was born and raised in Houston, Texas, where she still lives with her family.

Made in the USA
Columbia, SC
28 May 2022

60985121R00043